£2

Christmas 1994

For

Audrey

this beautiful
but
difficult book

H

Values

Collapse and Cure

Values
Collapse and Cure

Hailsham of St Marylebone

HarperCollins*Publishers*

HarperCollins*Publishers*
77–85 Fulham Palace Road,
Hammersmith, London W6 8JB

Published by HarperCollins*Publishers* 1994
1 3 5 7 9 8 6 4 2

A catalogue record for this book is
available from the British Library

ISBN 0 00 255390 2

Printed in Great Britain by
Butler & Tanner Ltd, Frome and London

Contents

I. Introduction.

The origin of this book lay in a mood of deep depression into which I fell towards the end of 1992. It happened to coincide with the hype about the Royal Family which was going on at the time. But it was not directly to do with that. At first I believed that my depression was due to the external political and economic situation. In part, no doubt, this triggered it off. I was deeply concerned with the stark contrast between the present state of my country and of the world as I perceived it in contemporary terms and the high hopes I had entertained for the future in 1945 when we entered on a period of peace after emerging victorious, and with an unstained reputation, after our conflicts with Hitler, Mussolini, and Japan. No doubt, I was also profoundly disappointed at the absence of improvement which had followed the collapse of Stalin's former empire in the late 1980's. Instead of the "peace dividend" which we had hoped for in our optimistic mood after the breach in the Berlin Wall, the civilised world seemed to be in a state of collapse due to fragmentation into separate and mutually antagonistic sub cultures. We had hoped for consolidation and progress under the leadership of the Western Democracies, and what we seemed to have achieved was mounting chaos. The world to which I had been deeply committed during a long, varied, and interesting life appeared to be crashing about my ears. Nor was the contrast between hopes unrealised and contemporary gloom confined to the international scene. It was not simply that the position of Britain, so universally admired in 1945, so unblemished in reputation after almost every other nation had either capitulated or joined the dark forces of tyranny and oppression, had so markedly declined. It seemed almost incredible that, after so much had been achieved in social welfare, in scientific and technical progress, and in international cooperation and organisation we should once again be gloomily confronted with the realities of recession and unemployment. I gradually became aware, however, that, whilst these things were certainly symptoms, and might easily have been the triggers which had produced my mood of doom and gloom, my actual despondency was due to a deeper underlying cause. It was a despondency about the failure of belief in the things which had buoyed me up throughout my life of nearly fourscore years and ten. It was not so much that I did not still hold them sacred in my own heart. It seemed to me that they were actually being obliterated from the operating motivation of mankind. I am not now talking about my religious beliefs as such. I do not expect such beliefs to be demonstrable. If they were demonstrable, the need for faith, and the duty to seek it would disappear. About three months before he died, my father had said to my stepsister, who was with him, rather strangely as I thought, and think: "I do not think it matters what one believes, as long as one believes in something". As a proposition, this is something with which I could not agree. Indeed, as a proposition, I regard it, taken literally, as nonsensical. My fundamental beliefs are personal, articulated and detailed, and I cannot see how I could hold them or any others like them if I did not believe them not merely to be true, but important, even when I have made full allowance for the certainty that, as a fallible human being, I cannot fail to have fallen into error about some of them, in whole or in part.

Nevertheless, there is a sense in which I cannot fail to sympathise with the sentiment even though I could not possibly accept the words in which my father chose to express it. Quite apart from the truths of religion, most, if not all, of which are indemonstrable, but in the validity and objective reality of which I believe it really important to have faith if one is to live one's life intelligently at all, even though one finds it difficult, even impossible to formulate in words the vision of it which in this life we see at best through a glass darkly, there is something else to be said. I refer to the world of values, and value judgments, the good, the right, the beautiful, the honourable, and even the true. I have come to see rather clearly that the darkening of the horizons of my own fin de siècle mood which I have been attempting to describe was not due to the external facts of life, like the situation in Bosnia or the Middle

East, or the existence of widespread depression or mass unemployment so much as the realisation that our vision of these things was becoming so confused and uncertain that people had really begun to believe that life was all a "tale told by an idiot, full of sound and fury" (or should I say theory) and signifying, quite literally, nothing. Stated baldly like this, the proposition seems so patently silly as not to be worth further consideration. But perhaps the fact that it was first stated in this language by our greatest English poet in one of the most moving of his tragedies should give us cause for further thought.

Certainly, it has had that effect on me. To begin with, I have reflected that there seems to be a body of persons, not amongst the most foolish, but amongst the cleverest men and women that I know, who appear not merely to believe just this, or something like it, but have actually taken the trouble to write extremely learned works to justify their conclusion. If I have understood it correctly, they would call this logical positivism, though I myself prefer to think of it as nihilism, that is that value judgments, by which I mean judgments about the reality of beauty, goodness, right, wrong, and the like are, quite literally non-sense, and, therefore, mean nothing at all, except in the sense that the grunts that an animal might give of approval or disapproval if you stroke it behind the ears or poke it in a tender spot with a stick, give one some idea of whether it is feeling pleasure, or the reverse.

Since then, I have come to reflect that, if this were true at the top end of the intellectual spectrum (that is, if, in the light or obscurity of nihilism, there can be an intellectual spectrum at all, or, if so, if it can have a top or bottom end) there is another body of persons who, at the bottom end, have exactly the same belief. These include the criminally minded, the feckless, the dwellers in cardboard boxes, the drug dependent, the violent, and a host of others. These also do not believe in the objective meaning in any of these value judgments at all. If this be true, it is something of a paradox that there should be this strange congruence between two such different classes of people, particularly since the point at issue is philosophical.

It is, I suppose, a point of view with which, at one moment or another, most of us in our lives have been confronted, and which most of us, at one time or another, have consciously rejected. But, stated in philosophical terms, the question at issue is: what is the status, what is the objective validity and what are the practical implications of the value judgments which we constantly make every time we speak of the true, the beautiful, the good, the right, the just, and, at the other end of the scale, the detestable, the ugly, the obscene, the cruel, and the unjust? Is this a question worth asking? And, if it is, what sort of an answer should we give? Obviously, the question is related to religion. But it is a philosophical and not a religious question. It is addressed to our reason and neither to our faith or want of it, nor to any revelation of the divine in human affairs.

II Value Judgments

Whatever the truth or falsity of value judgments, and whether they make sense or, as logical positivists would argue, quite literally, non-sense, that is mere subjective noises of approval or the reverse, they have meant a great deal to me. I do not believe that this admission convicts me of that most serious of the deadly sins, the sin of pride. I mean that values and judgments about them are precisely what has given meaning and purpose to my life. I have been proud of my country, Britain, or rather the British Isles. I have been proud of my mother's country, the United States, and of the part which, from the beginning, her family played in its history. I have been proud of the Church of England in the practice of whose faith I was brought up, and to which, after a brief and disastrous period of irreligion, I returned. Inside, and within, these and other loyalties there have been many more, to family and friends, to University and Colleges, to my profession, and after in 1939, I came to join them, the Army, and within the Army, my regiment. Less definite, and less tangible, there have been other values deriving from the

Western culture in whose traditions I was educated, and these have been no less influential: freedom, respect for law, authority, human dignity, freedom, moderation, justice, tradition, and a certain recognizable, but quite indefinable, sense of awe and ecstasy in the presence of beauty of colour, form, or sound, whether naturally created or humanly produced.

In the pride in my country which I have described I include, of course, its law, history, tradition, and achievements. While it still existed, I was proud of its empire, at one time covering about one quarter of the earth's inhabitable surface and population, and I was proud of the Commonwealth which succeeded it of independent sovereign peoples. I remain proud of our flexible constitution, including our so called monarchy (in fact we are a democratically governed republic with a wholly admirable hereditary Head of State, our independent judiciary, our Parliament of two Houses, and our ability to encompass diversity in unity and to carry on civilised debates about points of difference. Even the more horrible events of my lifetime, the two disastrous world wars, my revulsion at the tyrannies of Hitler and Stalin have tended only to strengthen my belief in, my love for and my loyalty to the institutions which I have been describing, and whose underlying cultures and beliefs I have tried to summarise. I am not now in the least ashamed of these loyalties which I do not consider in any way to have been inconsistent, foolish, or dishonourable. There have been many events which I did not foresee, and many developments which I did not welcome, and, of course, others ~~which~~ for which I had hoped but which did not occur. But nothing that I have experienced in a long and varied life of over fourscore years has dimmed my belief in an underlying view of the sanctities of human life, the nature and validity of which it is my purpose to analyse and defend. These sanctities extend beyond ethics and morality since, as I have said, they include all aesthetic judgments about beauty and ugliness. But they have this in common. Within each separate category a curious hierarchy of value on a scale varying between a qualitative top and a qualitative bottom. It is convenient to call the top end of the scale 'good', and the bottom end 'bad' or 'evil'. But these terms are not to be thought of as having a significance exclusively moral. We can speak of a 'bad' poem, or a 'bad' picture, and even a 'bad' quarto of Shakespeare without imputing any degree of moral disapproval. What is important is to note that there is a class of judgment in which we can express a judgment of quality, graded according to what is nearer or further from the top or bottom of a scale to which we attribute objective validity. It is convenient to call this category of expressed opinions 'value judgments'.

III Logical Positivism

By far the most numerous class of value judgment is that (or possibly we should say 'are those') related to human thoughts and actions. This class governs the whole field of moral philosophy, including all human behaviour to which ethical considerations apply. By extension, we might also assimilate political behaviour as well, since this must necessarily extend to much of law, political authority and jurisprudence. In themselves, value judgments are, of course, not exclusive to these fields. Most of us would include many of the aesthetic as ~~many~~ well as moral judgments. On the whole propositions to which only 'true' or 'false' would be appropriate belong to a different category. But the two fields overlap and there are frequent inconsistencies of treat, as when, as I have already observed, we classify Shakespeare's quartos or classical manuscripts as 'good' or 'bad' in accordance with the degree in which they contain true or false readings,

But the pages immediately following are principally concerned with those classes of value judgment strictly concerned with the ethical quality of human conduct, since it is with these that the school of logical positivism is principally and most characteristically concerned. The logical positivist regards these expressions of moral approval or disapproval as mere noises without objective meaning except as disclosing subjective movements of emotion on the part of those who utter them. As the late A.J. Ayer put it in his "Language, Truth and Logic"

"If I say to someone 'You acted wrongly in
"stealing that money', I am not
"saying anything more than if I
"had said: 'You stole that money.

"In adding that this action is wrong
"I am not making any further statement
"about it. I am simply evincing my
"moral disapproval of it. It is as if
"I had said: 'You stole that money'
"in a particular tone of horror, or
"written with the addition of
"some special exclamation marks.
" .... It merely serves to show
"that the expression of it is
"attended by certain feelings
"in the speaker".

This quotation from "Language, Truth, and Logic", made somewhat more fully in Iris Murdoch's

"Metaphysics as a guide to morals" contains the essence of what I mean by logical positivism, and I know, from personal conversation with the author, that this represents what he actually believed. I have already explained that I do not equate moral judgments with revealed religion. But it would be disingenuous to pretend that persons with religious convictions do not habitually use moral judgments in the form postulated by Ayer in a context that shows that they intend to convey a great deal more than the expression of purely subjective feelings of approval and disapproval. With the above passage from the late A.J. Ayer's probably most famous oeuvre, it is legitimate to contrast the words of St. Paul, writing to his converts in Philippi:

> "Finally, brethren, whatsoever things
> "are true, whatsoever things are honest,
> "whatsoever things are just, whatsoever
> "things are pure, whatsoever things
> "are lovely, whatsoever things are
> "of good report; if there be any
> " virtue, and if there be any praise,
> " think on those things".

This exactly illustrates my point. Of course, St. Paul certainly did not attempt to define or describe the things to which he was referring in using language of this kind. What is certain, however, is that he expected his readers to understand in general the kind of thing he meant, and that they had a validity altogether independent of his own purely subjective feelings which they would instinctively share with him.

In January 1903, rather more than four years before I was born, my grandfather was found one morning dead in his bath. He had been poisoned by a faulty geyser with carbon monoxide fumes. On his table in his study, according to my aunt's life of him, there was found an unfinished letter to one of his protegés in the Polytechnic which he had founded, who had obviously been troubled with religious difficulties and doubts. The letter contained these words:

> "Whatever else may be shaken, there
> "are some facts [sic] established
> "beyond the warrings of the theol-
> "ogians. Forever, virtue is better
> "than vice, truth than falsehood,
> "kindness than brutality".

Of course, one's first inclination is to criticise this generalisation for its apparent superfic-iality. To begin with, the use of the word 'facts' in the quotation begs the whole question which we are trying to discuss. Also it does not attempt to define or expand on what the doubter is intended to understand by 'virtue' or 'vice'. What is more important, however, is that, although he was probably referring to some conventionally accepted code of his time, my grandfather, like St. Paul, was evidently assuming that his reader would understand what he meant by the language he was using and that the words would be accepted by any fair minded person without regard to any purely subjective feelings of approval or disapproval peculiar either to the writer or the recipient. In the interesting and recently published book in which the above passage from Ayer's work is quoted somewhat more fully, "Metaphysics as a Guide to Morals", Iris Murdoch describes this particular aspect of logical positivism as expounded by Ayer, though "brilliant and ingenious" as "unsophisticated and dotty". But for my life long acquaintance with Ayer, I might have been disposed to agree, since I differed from Ayer in almost every judgment he ever made, though always affectionately disposed towards him. But whatever else Ayer was, the last thing I would have said about him, was that either he, or the young philosophers of his generation who shared his views, were either unsophisticated or dotty. They were, however, mesmerised by the works of the "Vienna Circle" and in particular of Ludwig Wittgenstein into accepting, hook, line, and sinker, the doctrine of logical positivism. In effect logical positivism exiles not only the whole of metaphysics, but almost all philosophical reasoning except their own into the realm of what its proponents deliberately chose to call non-sense. It would be idle and presumptuous on my part to attempt to explore all the origins and doctrines of the particular group, which, for a short period, captured the imagination of the generation of students almost immediately succeeding my own. In part, they were inspired by the work of the English empiricists, who, in their turn, caught their ideas partly from the collapse of the Aristotelian deductive logic so beloved by the medieval schoolmen. Rightly, they were impressed by the triumph of the founders of modern science ("natural philosophers") who were beginning to discover and expound the laws of the physical world by observation, measurement, calculation, and verification by experiment, and proceeded from this to general hypotheses which, even by their continuing refinement in the light of fresh experiment and observation, proved at best to be no more than provisional or incomplete. In this, the logical positivists were really only developing the underlying doctrines of Kant's 'Critique of Pure Reason' which claimed to demonstrate the virtual unknowability of 'Things in themselves' (Dinge an Sich) and the scepticism of David Hume. According to the Vienna circle, there were really only two classes of proposition. The first was 'analytic'. This included the truths of mathematics, and was so called because the material of the conclusion was already contained in the premises or axioms on which it was founded. Thus, in the ultimate analysis these were fundamentally tautologous in their nature. The second class of proposition consisted of the provisional hypotheses of the natural sciences. These were truly "synthetic" in that they reached genuinely new conclusions. But because, by definition, the conclusions contained new material not inherent in the original premises, they suffered from being forever provisional because all are inherently subject to modification or revision in the light of new observation and experimentation. Propositions which contained new assertions not, in this empirical sense, verifiable about the nature of reality or the universe and which were such that they were intrinsically incapable of verification or definition were described by logical positivists as, quite literally, non-sense, meaning that they were inherently incapable of any significant objective meaning. Thus, they consigned to the dustbin all the philosophical writings of Plato, much of Aristotle and all the preachings of the theologians. The only ancient philosophers who might have escaped this limbo of oblivion were the melancholy

Lucretius and the Epicureans, whose pessimistic and materialist opinions about the nature of the world and the limits of objective reality to some extent prefigured those of Wittgenstein and the Vienna circle.

I agree with Iris Murdoch that those conclusions are absurd but less because they are dotty or unsophisticated but because they are self contradictory. This is because, however it is formulated, the premise upon which the whole doctrine is based, namely that metaphysical doctrines and propositions, being incapable of verification, are ipso facto non-sense is itself a metaphysical proposition intrinsically incapable of verification. The logical positivists are, of course, on safe enough ground when they assert that the theories of science, being subject, at least in principle, to modification in the light of new observation and experiment, are also, at least in principle, provisional, and, since it is accepted that all scientific method presupposes observation, measurement, and experimental verification, it may readily be agreed that they are based on the systematic study of sense data. But even that is subject to one vital qualification. When confronted with the wonders of science, the pupils of one Oxford philosopher of my time, the late H.W.B. Joseph, were apt to point to the repeated and invariable fall of the apple in place of an even occasional upward movement, and to argue that this, in itself, was a valid reason for leading Newton to his formulation of the law of gravity. "Not at all" replied Joseph, "it should have caused him increasing surprise". So, clearly, it should were it not for the fact that human beings have what Locke might have called an innate idea that the universe makes sense and that causality is one way, and perhaps the only way, of making sense out of one class of observations which are evidently not self explanatory. If this were not so Newton and the natural philosophers of our age would have to be consigned, with Plato and the others, to the same limbo.

So much for logical positivism. It fails because it is self contradictory.

IV. The Tao

The way is now open to discuss the validity or the reverse of our value judgments. Obviously, even in the case of the physical sciences, we cannot climb out of the restrictive framework of time and space which conditions all our thoughts, whether about the nature of the physical world and its contents or even the language in which we describe them or theorise about them. The medievalists believed that new knowledge could be obtained by the process of deduction, that is, the drawing of new conclusions from old premises which for them meant par excellence the inspiration of the Old and New Testaments and the infallible teachings of the Church. Various attempts were made to substitute premises somewhat more compelling than these, and more conformable to the actual experience of mankind. Descartes made the brave but unsuccessful attempt to deduce much new knowledge from his "cogito ergo sum" that is the facts of consciousness and the process of ratiocination themselves. Perhaps more realistically, the English empiricists, notably Berkeley, Locke, and Hume, recognized that new knowledge had in fact been derived from the systematic study of sense data. But they failed to understand that the processes of reasoning assumed in the study of phenomena were themselves intrinsically non phenomenal. This led some, like Berkeley, to question the existence of physical matter altogether, thus leading Samuel Johnson to kick a stone with his famous: "Sir, I refute it thus." In the end it brought Hume and, later, Kant to a complete scepticism as to whether we could know anything at all about "things in themselves", since all we had to go by were the sense data we received and not a direct apprehension of the things at all. Going even further, Kant went on from his "pure" to his "practical" reason to postulate the existence of God from the "categorical imperative" of the human conscience. It took a long time for people to realise that it is not possible to use reason itself as a critique to justify the validity of our reasoning process itself. Knowledge grows like a plant out of our reasoning process and our ability to formulate conclusions and hypotheses from its exercise. But it does not arise by the processes of syllogistic deduction postulated by Thomas Aquinas or Aristotle, nor, simply, by the examination and enumeration of instances ("induction") ingeniously suggested by Francis Bacon in his ambitiously entitled "Novum Organum", named after Aristotle's famous work. Such a mere examination of instances should, as Joseph pointed out to his pupils, have caused him "increasing surprise". Nevertheless, apart from Haldane, Bacon was the one Lord Chancellor who made a positive contribution to philosophical thought. He had hit on the fact that new "knowledge" grows out of experience, more like a plant than the solution of a "three pipe problem" by Sherlock Holmes, and that "knowledge" so obtained consists at the best in provisional hypotheses subject to constant revision, refinement, and modification. The truth, which the logical positivists failed to appreciate, is that, however hard you try, you cannot validate your process of reasoning by the very processes you are trying to validate. Now we see through a glass, darkly. It remains true, however, that, in our human condition, it is the only way in which we can see at all. Recognizing this as a limitation, I find this a liberating rather than a humiliating thought. If I proceed to discuss the objective validity of value judgments, I do not feel myself in any way to be talking non-sense, since, although they assume the existence of consiousness and sense perception, these are not the primary subjects under discussion. As between St. Paul and my grandfather on one side of the intellectual boxing ring and A.J. Ayer and Wittgenstein on the other, I stand foursquare with St. Paul and Quintin Hogg, and I am not conscious of anti-intellectualism if, changing my metaphor, I boldly kick a stone and, with Samuel Johnson, exclaim: "Sir, I refute it thus".

The point I now make was well made in a passage, which I will quote, from A.N. Wilson's biography of C.S. Lewis. The point is the manifest congruence between men and women of vastly differing cultures, languages, and religions on certain points, of, to me, overriding significance, particularly in the field of conduct but not less in the appreciation of beauty. In his discussion of the work entitled "The Abolition of Man", A.N. Wilson wrote:

"Lewis' contention, which cannot historically
"be denied, was that there has been a
"system of values discernible in almost all
"moral and religious centres from the
"beginning of literature until the mid
"twentieth century. To emphasise that
"he was not just talking about the

"Judaeo-Christian tradition, but something
" much deeper and wider than that, Lewis
" borrowed the Chinese word and called this
" the Tao. In an appendix quoting from
" sources as varied as the Old Norse Voluspa,
" the Ancient Egyptian 'Confession of a
" Righteous Soul, the Chinese Analects,
" Cicero and Epictetus, he makes his point.
" 'They all point to the existence outside
" individual feelings or the purely utilit-
" arian requirements of a society, something
" which can be termed a generally
" accepted standard of right and wrong.
" All these sources abhor murder,

" dishonesty, theft, unkindness, disregard
" of the old, cruelty to children, ruthless
" 'justice' untempered by mercy".

This perception of the world of values was important to Lewis, as it had been to my grandfather because, despite the obvious failure of the verification principle, despite the enormous differences between individual groups from time to time, despite the failure to define what exactly is meant, it reflects a firm belief that there is something in human nature, wherever found, and derived from whatever source, which asserts the objective validity of value judgments concerning conduct. This assertion can be shown empirically to be true independently of all human failings and fallibility, of all individually differing analyses, and independently of the existence of all rival ideologies. Let anyone who has felt what I can only describe as the sense of ecstasy at the sight of a beautiful dawn or sunset, or the night sky in the mountains or the desert, or even the brilliant flash of green in the plumage of a quite ordinary bird, or even the breath taking wonder at the creations of human art dare to assert that he is condemned to eternal silence on the reality of his feelings if he cannot quite find words to express his feelings, or warn himself that if he makes the attempt he will be talking non-sense, and I will contradict him to his face. In my grandfather's terms I would say that anyone who has lived through the age of Hitler or Stalin, the Holocaust of the Jews, or the Katyn massacres, try to say seriously that there is no difference in value or meaning between kindness and brutality, or truth and falsehood, or virtue and vice, and I will tell him to his face that it is he who is talking non-sense and that he will find no reputable or intelligent human being to join him. It does not matter whether one delves into the past and any serious ancient philosophies, or studies any or all past or present religions, Buddhist, Muslim, Hindu, Christian or pagan. All would stand with my grandfather and St. Paul against the logical positivist. We may be uneasily aware that neither the physical, moral, or aesthetic world is fully self explanatory to human beings. But what is the true non-sense is to assert that there is no difference in principle between beautiful and ugly, cruel and kind, honest and dishonest, good and bad, right and wrong, and that in asserting the contrary and claiming an objective reality and meaning to these opposites of comparison we are simply making subjective noises designed to show that they are attended by certain sensations individual to the speaker.

The importance of this is not merely theoretical, but has enormous practical significance. I can do no better than to conclude with a second summation by A. N. Wilson in the same biography of C. S. Lewis from which I have quoted above. If it does not diminish the occasional fits of despondency which I began by confessing it begins at least to make clear what is wrong. It is a loss of a sense of values. This is how A. N. Wilson sums up the argument. He writes as follows:

"In his short book ["The Abolition of Man"]
"Lewis does not elaborate on what
" remedies there can be which will save
" the world from the effects of exploitation
" by a comparatively few unscrupulous
" people. Those who identify Lewis'
" fears solely with the Nazi experiments
" might consider that the world has
" become a better place since 1944,
" and that he was exaggerating. But
" the whole growth since that period
" of ecology, about the calamitous
" consequences of viewing the earth
" merely as a thing to be exploited

"by man its master gives the lie to this.
"Lewis' arguments cover the proliferation
"of nuclear arsenals, the so called advance
"of medical science in the area of
"experimenting on human embryos,
"the effect on Third World countries
"of such fruits of enlightenment as
"modern baby food and aerosol sprays.
"His diagnosis of the disease cannot
"be lightly dismissed. In 'The
"'Abolition of Man' he does not
"advance the cure, though there is
"no secret where he thought it lay
"if there was one."

Though I agree with its general drift, this is not a passage which I would have written myself. Despondency of a more general kind about the trends in modern Britain and more generally in the post war world is not confined to the ecological examples given. Still less, however, is it a purely subjective hallucination in the mind of an ageing lawyer and politician. It is the condemnation of a world which has neglected or denied the moral judgments which, in his pilgrimage through history, man dimly perceives and insufficiently appreciates. Unless he wishes to perish utterly, he must learn that life is not a "tale told by an idiot, signifying nothing". It is governed by laws which it is within the natural powers of a normal human being to study, learn, and faithfully obey. "Forever virtue is better than vice, truth than falsehood, kindness than brutality". This is a truth which we ignore only at our peril. It is also one which may hold one of the keys to our understanding of the Universe. The verification principle as formulated and applied by the logical positivists is not only false but dangerously misleading. There is a system of values, open to perception by those who conscientiously seek it, incapable of verification, not open to exact definition or formulation. To speak about them, to debate them and to pursue them is not the non-sensical activity which the logical positivists claim them to be. It is obvious that they approach the very frontiers of thought, and, therefore, of language, for words fail when we approach the throne of the ineffable. But this should not prevent us from rejecting categorically the positivist dictum: "That of which we cannot speak is something concerning which we are compelled to be silent". (Das wovon man nichts sprechen kann, darüber muss man schweigen). We are not condemned to perpetual silence in meditation on the Tao. We are embarking on a necessary pilgrimage of the spirit.

V Aesthetic Judgments.

Hitherto, the argument has been designed around two cognate but separate propositions. The first is that, inherent in human nature there exists what Locke might have described as a single innate idea. But it is not, in the ordinary sense, an idea. The universe as it is unveiled to us in our experience of it from the cradle to the grave is not self explanatory. Nevertheless, we have an invincible craving to make sense of it. From the moment when the baby begins to take stock of his surroundings to the moment when, as a mature adult who has become a scientist, he formulates a new theory, the same irresistible process is at work, telling him that the world of his experience makes sense and that his reasoning process applied to his observation, measurements, calculations, and experiments will help him to make such sense. But, paradoxically, nothing will validate the reasoning process itself. This is logically impossible because our scientist's use of the reasoning process antedates the discoveries to which it gives rise. He may be reassured when he utilises his mathematical reason and finds a coherence between what he has been taught and others have learned before him, or continue to find when they conjoin with him in his studies. He will also be reassured when he learns that the theories which he has formulated, instead of "causing him increasing surprise" enable him to predict with accuracy the future results of new experiments. He may be disconcerted if these go wrong and produce results different from his expectation. In the last case, still using the same reasoning power, he will work back along the course which he has travelled, to see where he has gone astray. But the one thing he cannot validate is the reasoning power itself. If it confirms his theories, he will persist in using the same processes of thought to conquer fresh fields of discovery and formulate new hypotheses. But he will also know that all may be subject to the same liability to refinement, correction or revision as he goes along. If he makes errors of reasoning or observation, as he will from time to time, he will travel back along his course, still using the same reasoning process and still assuming its validity until he first finds, and then corrects his mistake. From the first, he knows that the world which he is experiencing is not self explanatory, and to the end he relies on his reasoning process to discover part of the explanation. But in no case can he validate the reasoning process itself.

There are, however, more kinds of experience than one which will result from his presence in the world of time and space. His increasing knowledge of mathematics is logically self contained as conclusions follow inexorably from premises and axioms. His increasing work on particle accelerators or whatever other apparatus he employs to will lead him on from hypothesis to hypothesis. But it will not validate the growing coherence of his experience, because he has no alternative but to rely on it. But there is another class of experience of which this is not true. He will be subject to the same difficult choices of conduct as the test of us. Some of these will contain a moral element. Some will not, as, for instance, when he has to choose between two apparently equally attractive offers of appointment. But, more analogous to any moral choices that he has to make, there will be a third class of judgments which he will be called upon to make, which have more congruence with his moral than his practical choices or his mathematical calculations. These will be the class of his aesthetic preferences. He may be amazed by the beauty of the rising or setting sun, delighted at the charm of one painting or disgusted at the ugliness of another. These aesthetic judgments will have no moral content and no moral effects upon his behaviour. But, in contradistinction to his scientific hypotheses which can be modified or revised by further measurement or experiment, and to his mathematical calculations which can be checked precisely, these aesthetic judgments can only be discussed or debated in comparison with those made by other people, some of whom may be more worthy of respect than others. What is important about the aesthetic judgments is that, though they have no intrinsic moral quality at all, they possess the same sort of hierarchy of value as do moral judgments, and the only way of checking their validity or otherwise is to see whether there is the same sort of congruence between persons of wisdom and experience as that which we have observed in the Tao. It is this possibility of congruence or divergence which enables critics to discuss Milton and Shakespeare, Pheidias and Praxiteles, or, for that matter, Beatrix Potter and Enid Blyton. The importance of aesthetic judgments and their quite different scales of value is to reassure us that the presence or absence of admitted and definable criteria is not necessarily a bar to a belief in an objective validity underlying judgments of this kind.

As will be seen later, in the field of law, for instance, one difficulty in the way of accepting or rejecting the scale of acceptable values which, in our instance of law, law is expected to embody, one seems to lose oneself immediately in a mass of casuistry. Take, for instance, the prohibitions in the Ten Commandments. At first sight "Thou shalt not kill" seems so simple, so completely satisfying, indeed so obvious. But examine it a little more closely and it quickly seems to disappear into a sort of fog. The Prayer Book version: "Thou shalt do no murder" is only a little clearer. How much force is one entitled to use in defence of others or of self, and in what circumstances? What is the intention necessary to constitute the sin? What degree of instability exonerates? Do we include abortion in the prohibition and if so at what stage after fertilisation and are there exceptions, and, if so, what are they? Is "mercy killing" within the prohibition, and, if so, in what circumstances? What is the appropriate penalty? There are many more questions, none easily answered, and many, if not all, degenerate on analysis, into questions of degree on which argument can be unending, and refinements of casuistry unnumbered. It is necessary at times to take a firm grip on oneself and to remind one's common sense that the original prohibition contains an obvious moral truth which exists in spite of all the casuistry, and that all civilised countries prohibit homicide if not in all cases at least in some, often with separate degrees of guilt, and most agree that the degree of moral guilt depends on a moral state rather than on the success or failure of the enterprise. I find it extremely helpful to remind myself that the moral judgments come in a large number of categories with widely varying implications of praise and blame, and that some value judgments, particularly those which I have designated as aesthetic, like the appreciation of a beautiful landscape or a lovely piece of music, have no practical consequences at all in terms of human behaviour. It is also worth remembering that some moral judgments, perhaps the most important of which is: "Greater love hath no man than this" contain nothing but praise and no element of censure at all. Belief in the objective validity of aesthetic judgments is thus a strong reinforcement of my belief in the objective validity of our ethical perceptions.

VI Values in Law

Whereas the natural sciences are concerned with theories about facts, and their tools and methods, observation, measurement, calculation, experiment and hypothesis, values are essentially about what the late A: J: Ayer happily described as 'hooray words' and 'boo words'. Contrary to his views, I am arguing that these are not merely words, but significant statements with objective meanings which can command rational acceptance or rejection. Aesthetic judgments, which I have just discussed, are particularly instructive because they contain no ethical content, although the 'hooray' and the 'boo' elements are, of course, both present and recognisable. Logically, perhaps, the present chapter might be expected to deal with private morality, the 'hooray' and 'boo' elements in which apply without external sanctions. But man is a social animal. He exists in groups ranging from husband and wife through an infinitely large number of the so-called 'little platoons' to the nation state, and, beyond the nation state, into an international stratosphere. To all these groups, judgments involving 'hooray' and 'boo' elements apply, and, since it is the fundamental element in human society governing normative human conduct, perhaps it is as well to start with law, arguably the first of the social sciences.

At first sight the origin of law is pragmatic. Historically English law seems to be based on the idea of "the King's peace". But this is only an idiosyncratic way of recognizing that in all secular societies, whether primitive or more sophisticated, the secular sovereign claims a monopoly, or, more accurately, a near monopoly, of the use of force. It is curious how this fact has given rise among philosophers to definitions of law which contain no ethical content at all. Law, like metaphysics, possesses its own group of logical positivists. It is, of course, not surprising that, in authoritarian writings, this should be so. "Law", the Nazi régime claimed, is what pleases the Führer". (Das ist Recht was dem Führer gefällt). But this claim does not differ in principle from what was asserted by the nineteenth century, and liberal, author, Austin. "Law", said he, "is the Command of the Ruler". His twentieth century, and, I believe unrelated, namesake, the late J. L. Austin was more circumspect.

"If you could get a collection of

"more or less cantankerous colleagues

"all to accept something after argument,

"that would be a bit of a criterion".

It is fair, however, to admit that, in that context, he was not talking specifically about law, but, more generally, about philosophical correctness. Herbert Hart, something of a philosopher as well as a lawyer, is, rightly or wrongly, credited with the somewhat enigmatic observation that: "Law is what the Courts will decide", a definition which, whatever else it contains, has neither 'boo' nor 'hooray' element attached to it.

There is a good deal to be said for

this school of legal positivists. It is certainly convenient for the practitioner. But it hardly exhausts the discussion. Given that, in all organised societies, the secular authority claims a near monopoly of the use of force, two conclusions follow. The first is that the authority must publish a more or less coherent set of rules informing members of the public in response to what sorts of conduct the direct use of force is to be expected. Otherwise chaos will undoubtedly ensue. But the second consequence is of more far reaching practical importance. If the state is to operate a near monopoly of the use of force, it has to take upon itself the responsibility for the peaceful settlement of all private disputes which might lead individuals to use violence themselves as a means of self help. The result of these two necessities gives rise to the entire code of law, from the legal complexities of "Bleak House" to the somewhat simpler provisions which led two of Henry VIII's six wives to the executioner's block on Tower Hill.

The real weakness of all definitions of law by the positivist school is that all are entirely vacuous. They fail to answer the question posed by Aristotle when he discussed what he called the final cause. The question is: What is it for? What is law for? What constitutes a good law? How does it differ from a law which is bad? Many have given different answers and no doubt will continue to do so. But it is clear that no answer is possible without addressing the issue of values. With Plato and Socrates, out of sheer practical necessity we are driven to ask, and attempt to answer the question: "What is justice?" Justice is the principle which Parliament claims to apply when it passes every year its thousands of pages of public general Acts. It is the principle by which Ministers seek to defend their tens of thousands of pages of Statutory Instruments, Orders in Council, directions to local authorities, and so on and so on. However difficult or easy to give some account of the matter in the relatively simple societies of the Greek City states of the fifth and fourth centuries BC or in the infinitely more complex societies of the twentieth and twenty first centuries AD, it is impossible to attempt an answer without a wide range of "boos" and "hoorays" formulated in a series of value judgments all of which are based on some principles of morality. To say simply, even with absolute formal veracity, that law is what the Courts will decide is simply to evade the question of what law, in all its diverse patterns, and complicated minuets is all about.

Of course, attempts are made to simplify the subject. Moses appears to have thought that the essence of the matter could be inscribed on two tablets of stone, which indeed shed a good deal of light on the subject even to this day. In his more or less successful jousts with the traditionalist Blackstone, Jeremy Bentham launched his famous Utilitarian formula: "The greatest happiness of the greatest number is the foundation of morals and legislation". But, whether as a formula for morals, or, what is more relevant to the present discussion, for legislation, this definition, which still has its adherents, is one of the most defective ever proposed. I pass by the sterile point that, of all the 'hooray' words ever invented, 'happiness' is probably the most subjective and capable of almost endless philosophical and casuistical dispute. I concede without argument that in many, perhaps most, cases the common good or the general welfare must take precedence over individual preferences. An obvious instance would be the rule of the road for the drivers of vehicles. There are also obvious instances drawn from purely private morality when we heap the warmest praise on men who willingly sacrifice their lives to save those of their friends, like the member of Scott's Antarctic expedition who left the relative protection of his tent for the subzero temperatures and conditions outside. Nevertheless, no one with any sense of justice or morality can reduce these noble examples to mere questions of measurement, as to how you can compare one 'happiness' in quality or quantity against another. Nor can either be a question of counting heads. The greatest happiness of the greatest number" denies that justice may ever assert the rights of a dissentient minority, or even a dissentient individual, against a powerful or intolerant majority, or an unpopular against a popular opinion. Though I am no great proponent of lists of 'natural', 'human' or 'inherent' rights, the founders of American independence were surely right, if philosophically naïve, when they claimed that life, liberty and the pursuit of happiness in the individual, if not actually 'inalienable' at least ought to have some precedence over the command of the ruler or the preference of an anonymous majority. Whatever defects may be discerned in their Declaration of Independence, there was, at least, no crude reduction of the rights of the individual to mere measurement and the counting of heads. It is impossible to eliminate the concepts of morality and individual rights from any just or even rational idea of law. Let Bentham pontificate as he might, and did, about 'natural rights' being 'nonsense on stilts', and, whatever status one chooses to give to the Universal Declaration or European Convention on human rights, I would defend to the last my own conviction that one of the main purposes of law and justice, courts, judges, Governments and Parliaments is to protect the weak against the strong, the few, and even, in extreme cases, the individual, against the many, the unpopular against the popular. The 'greatest happiness of the greatest number' may serve well enough as a slogan. But, in a democracy, it becomes a charter for elective dictatorship, the denial of justice in the interests of a shifting and perhaps amoral majority. If nonsense walks on stilts it is under the banner of populist utilitarianism, and not of natural, that is individual, or minority rights.

It is, however, one thing to assert that law cannot be divorced from minority rights or morality. But it is a totally different thing to attempt to divorce law from the facts and limits of the practicable in favour of some starry eyed ideal. Societies differ geographically and historically. They differ enormously in composition, in social and economic organisation, in the balance between town and country. C.S. Lewis' perception of the Tao, a congruence of wise opinions joining continents, cultures, and religious and ethnic divisions, has its force in the field of moral philosophy. But lawyers and legislators have to keep their feet firmly on the ground. In any given society, the laws cannot afford not to pay due attention to the degree of industrial development, the moral and social perceptions and habits, the ethnic and religious affiliations, and all the other characteristics of the populations whose conduct they seek to regulate. In actuality, and to be at all enforceable, it is probable that law should prescribe standards of conduct considerably better than the worst, and lower noticeably than the best performance of the society expected to obey it. The best definition of law standing on the lowest stilts I can describe is that law is natural morality translated into the enforceable.

VII Values and private morality

Clearly, my first task is to defend the title of this chapter. Surely, it will be argued, I should have put private morality in front of law, if only because I have claimed that law is in some sense derived from the values of private morality and not vice versa.

The short answer to this is that this is exactly what I have tried to do. Before even tentatively approaching the topic of law, I tried to show that, so far from natural duties and rights being nonsense on stilts, there is a congruence between the wise of all nations, cultures and languages as to the way in which all human beings ought to behave, and that C. S. Lewis had given to this congruence of opinion the Chinese name of the Tao. Another name might have been 'natural morality'. I next sought to analyse the idea of law, and drew the conclusion that, in its very nature, law is natural morality translated in any given society into the enforceable. But this pragmatic view now needs to be further examined. Despite Lord Atkin's famous reference in a leading case in the House of Lords to the lawyer's question in St. Luke's Gospel: "Who is my neighbour?"

(which elicited the parable of the Good Samaritan) there is no law, so far as I know, either in England or in any other civilised country which enacts the precept: "Thou shalt love thy neighbour as thyself". Still less is there any definition of 'neighbour' which would pass the scrutiny of the Parliamentary draftsman. There is yet a further qualification which must be made. "Thou shalt love thy neighbour as thyself" is not a rule of conduct at all. It is a quotation from Leviticus which prescribes motivation underlying the precepts embodied in the law and justifying their enactment. A further qualification is demanded by the parable itself. Even though it were a rule of conduct enacted by law, it is not possible to give a satisfactory legal definition of 'neighbour'. In the parable, it was shown to refer to the relation of two perfect strangers who met fortuitously on the road to Jericho, even though they belonged to two mutually hostile communities. In Lord Atkin's case, he again applied it to the relation between two perfect strangers. They had never met at all. One had bought a bottle of ginger beer which the other had manufactured and which had been sold to the purchaser by an intermediate retailer.

Though, in the parable, the precept was shown to apply to two members of different communities, in Leviticus it describes the relationship governed by a code of conduct designed to be both legal and moral imposed on members of a Chosen People with one another and those outside their number with whom they came into contact. Both on the lips of Paul of Tarsus and of the Author of the parable, the precept was to be second and subordinate to a belief in a transcendent Being to whom alone absolute devotion was reserved. It was part of a metaphysical religion, and not of a civil or criminal code of law in the modern sense at all. In Bentham's derogatory language, such beliefs are not merely "nonsense on stilts" but one of a number of

> "imaginary laws fancied and
> "invented by poets, rhetoricians,
> "and dealers in moral and
> "intellectual poisons ... imaginary
> "rights, a bastard brood of
> "monsters"

In this kind of atmosphere, Humpty Dumpty's views of language and reality might be thought to reign supreme

At this stage, I must make an apology. In what I am writing here, I am deliberately seeking to exclude purely religious or theological beliefs, whether my own or anyone else's. This is because I believe that philosophy has a word to say which must be heard and received in the light of reason unaided by theology or religion. But here we are on borderline territory. The discovery of the Tao as perceived by C.S. Lewis led him, as it has me, to a belief in Theistic religion, and, beyond Theism, to the Christian faith. But in C.S. Lewis' case, as in mine, the belief in what he called 'the Tao', and I 'natural morality' pre-existed in his mind to any religion and may, therefore, be discussed in isolation from any theological implications. These may, or may not, be read into it, or deduced from it. For psychological rather than logical reasons there may have been some causal relation in their progress. That this is at least theoretically possible may be clearly seen from the fact that Cicero, the Roman orator and author, who died forty three years before the traditional date for the opening of the Christian era, and had, so far as is known, no serious acquaintance with Hebrew literature or religion, was able to write in his philosophical treatise on law:

"We (that is, the human race) have a natural propensity to love our fellowmen, which is the foundation of all law". (Natura propensi sumus ad diligendos homines, quod fundamentum juris est. De legibus I·43). It remains true, however, that many of us who struggle to make sense of a universe which is not self explanatory, have found it difficult to stop at a belief in natural morality, and have gone on to postulate from it the existence of a transcendental Absolute, union with which is the ultimate object and end of our pilgrimage. There is, however, no logical necessity to proceed thus far.

What is necessary is to recognize the objective validity of a natural morality, even though it is incapable of definition per genus et speciem and even though the rules for its performance cannot be listed and catalogued on the analogy of ten, or any other number of, Commandments. Such catalogues and precepts may be sign posts to help us on our way and control our passage through the world of space and time. But they cannot be used as lamp posts to support our instability. Just as the law should be the rules of natural morality translated into the enforceable in the light of the actualities of Society, so there is an analogous reduction in the field of morality itself in the light of valid but conflicting claims and factual complexities with which the individual conscience finds itself confronted. The commandments of private morality spread both more widely and less precisely than the terms in which they can be most easily expressed.

VIII Morality and the practicable

I hope that there will have been little if any disagreement with me when I have claimed that law is not a series of precepts and prohibitions corresponding exactly to an ideal code of morality but must make concessions to enforceability and the realities of the society in which it is to be applied. But more eyebrows may be raised in surprise when I claim that a somewhat analogous rule must be conceded about the applicability of ideal morality to individual conduct. Such a claim is not a dangerous concession to the theory of moral relativism. In the first place, there may be legitimate but conflicting moral claims on the activities of the same individual and there are occasions when he will have to choose between them. Sometimes the necessity for choice is obvious. In general, for instance, it is obviously wrong to break a promise. But there must be few who would not accept a summons to sit beside the bed of a sick or injured wife or child rather than keep an important social or public engagement. In the parable of the Good Samaritan no doubt all three characters who noticed the victim lying by the roadside had important business to transact in Jericho which might well have involved the convenience or rights of some third party. But the good Samaritan rightly judged that these must yield to the urgent need for help of the injured stranger. Similarly, in the Prodigal Son the elder brother had a legitimate grievance against his father for not allowing him to give parties to his friends in the parental home. But the return of the Prodigal despite all his past behaviour was rightly seen to take precedence over the legitimate grievance. In the Alternative Service Book of the Church of England it seems at one point to be suggested that every faithful Christian is under an absolute obligation to subordinate his own rights and interest to an abstraction called the Common Good. But it does not need a very clever casuist to point to occasions when the rights of other individuals or even the individual's own good might take precedence over that abstraction. Indeed, if taken quite literally the precept might well prove inconsistent with the requirements of the Golden Rule. This prescribes that we should love our neighbour as, but not better than, oneself. What is prohibited by it is to build a sort of hierarchy of rights and interests with one's own at the top and those of one's neighbours lower down in the scale of importance. The occasions may be rare. But there must be some rights of one's own which in some circumstances one is entitled to protect against all comers. Practicability must also carry some weight in governing the choice between alternative courses of action. Often, of course, it is one's duty to attempt the difficult or the dangerous to assist a neighbour. But no one can be under an obligation to attempt the impossible. Without accepting in the least the doctrine of relativity in moral values, in concrete situations, morality, like law must have some element of practical possibilities as perceived at the time for action by the prospective agent. It may never be correct to preach that the end justifies the means. But from time to time it must be correct to argue that, of two possible courses, each likely to be attended by undesirable consequences, it is right to choose the one likely to bring about the lesser evil. Often enough, of course, morality can be correctly depicted as a stark choice between right and wrong, and often enough, alas, we choose the latter. Nevertheless, some allowance must be made for human error, and, to some extent, moral choices are always obscured by our inability to predict the future. Particularly when we are passing judgment on the conduct of others, it is a safe rule to remember the precept: "Judge not that ye be not judged".

IX Values and Secular Authority

All organised societies, all codes of law, and all treatises on ethics, recognize some obligation to obey the secular authorities of the state, and all civilised codes of law and theories of morality and religion in practice admit that there must be some limits to the right of the sovereign to demand, and the duty of the subject to concede obedience. But it is, and will always remain a subject of perpetual dispute amongst intelligent men and women to define the extent and the limits in each case. If for this reason only, it is worth while to mount a discussion on this subject as an appendix, as it were, to our accounts of values in law and in private morality which we have just ended. The questions raised are closely related to both, inseparable indeed. Nevertheless they demand separate treatment.

Writing in the thirteenth century, Bracton, the earliest of the classical English jurists, defended the doctrine that the titular Sovereign could not be impleaded in his own Courts by saying that he "is under God and the law". Unhappily this begs both important questions, namely the identity of the legitimate Sovereign and the inherent limitations on all secular authority, questions artfully dodged by the Founder of the Christian religion when questioned about the propriety of paying tribute to the occupying power in Roman occupied Palestine.

Neither question is always easy of solution. In the Wars of the Roses, with the representatives of York and Lancaster occupying the English throne almost alternately, the identity of the legitimate sovereign proved so difficult of solution by the individual subject that Parliament wisely provided that no treason was committed if he chose to obey the King who happened to be occupying the throne at the time, notwithstanding in any defect in title which might subsequently appear. I believe this pragmatic sanction still to represent the law. The long debate about the legitimacy of the Hanoverian succession produced some cynical epigrams in the 18th century:

Thus: "Treason can never prosper. What's the reason./ If treason prosper none dare call it treason"

Or: "God save the King (I mean the Faith's defender./God bless (no harm in blessing) the Pretender/. But who Pretender is, and who the King (God bless my soul) is quite another thing."

But, quite apart from the difficulty of identifying the legitimate sovereign, men will argue for ever about the point at which disobedience becomes a duty and ceases to be a crime, and the point at which the right (or duty) of rebellion begins or ceases against a tyrannical regime whose whole rule has become insupportable. Those of us who have watched from afar the tyrannies of Hitler or Stalin can well see the reasons for the debate, and, even under an elective government, the point can theoretically arise when secular authority, however legitimate in origin, has to be condemned as elective dictatorship and the moral authority of its pronouncements becomes disputable. On the one point, few people would support the idea that, simply because one rightly disapproved Hitler's régime, one would have been entitled to disobey the traffic police who sought in Nazi Germany to regulate the flow of traffic at a cross roads. Indeed, there is Biblical authority for this. When the author of St. Peter's Epistles enjoined his converts to "honour the King" he meant Nero, no less. On the other hand it will be a matter of perennial controversy at what point and in respect of what matters "civil disobedience" becomes defensible and ceases to be a public nuisance..

But this is exactly the point at which casuistry begins and debate becomes both futile and unending. From Magna Carta to the American Bill of Rights, from Hobbes' Leviathan to David Hume, and continuing to this day attempts have been made to define catalogues of 'rights' declared to be 'fundamental' or 'inalienable' or claiming to have discovered some general philosophical principle justifying or condemning disobedience on the one hand or repression on the other. In the aftermath of World War II international attempts were made to formulate codes of behaviour governing the conduct of governments and the rights of the subject. Such is the United Nations Charter, the Universal Declaration of Human Rights, and the European Convention on the same with its various protocols. All attempt to lay down acceptable codes for the prevention of oppression and aggression and the protection of individuals. None are without value, and, as guidelines, all have served some useful purpose. If I now attempt some generalisations not contained, or containable in these codes, I do so only in the knowledge that they are not designed for tablets of stone. The first is that all behaviour must have regard to the general rules of natural morality as perceived by civilised opinion at the time. The second is that the burden of justifying any breach of the peace whether by individuals or secular authorities must lie heavily on those who seek to defend it. The third, which follows from the second, is that the so-called principle of proportionality should be rigidly adhered to, that is, that no more force should be used than is judged reasonably necessary to achieve the just result, and, conversely, that the result aimed at should have a degree of importance proportionate to the force needed in the attempt to achieve it. The art of the possible extends to the field of morality as well as politics.

X The International Dimension

The last discussion began with an examination of the duty owed by the individual to secular authority. But it led inexorably to a new dimension in our discussion of the role of value judgments. Governments do not exist in a vacuum. Their relationships are not simply with individuals and the "little platoons". They exist in a world peopled by other governments, and this international dimension, though always present, has emerged with increasing insistence since the end of the last war. My father always used to contend that, in the true sense of the word, there was no such thing as international law. Naturally enough, this was not a view to commend itself greatly to international lawyers. After all there has been a huge literature on the subject ever since, in the seventeenth century, Grotius expatiated on the jus gentium, which, according to him, dictated the ethics of international behaviour.

But this was not quite what my father had meant. On analysis, the jus gentium seems increasingly similar to the state of nature which, in his "Leviathan" Hobbes contended would govern the conduct of individuals, were there no Sovereign in existence to keep them in order. When my father was in his prime, international society consisted primarily of independent sovereign states, some governed by individuals, and some with more developed liberal constitutions. Between these, there was no conception comparable to what, in an earlier chapter, I referred to as "the King's peace". There was no international executive, no real international legislature. International relations were governed by custom or by treaty. True, some of these were international like the Geneva Convention or the League of Nations Covenant, and a wide network of other arrangements, both bilateral and multilateral. But all these sovereign states could denounce or disregard. There was no adequate means of enforcement, except by the recently established Hague Court, whose jurisdiction was similarly based on treaty, and which had no forces at its command. There existed, of course, a body of customary rules, known by courtesy as International Law. These included the International Law of War, governing the conduct of belligerents and neutrals, and a rather vaguer set of rules, the International Law of Peace, which was supposed to regulate the conduct of governments so long as they remained technically at peace with one another. But, although the moralists and theologians had written volumes about what constituted a "Just War", which was intended to restrain the conduct of independent states before they became belligerent, there was no effective international agency (apart from the League of Nations Covenant) with actual power to impose or define any restraints upon their actual power to do so.

This was not because the need for such an agency had not been recognized. There was, for instance, a conception known as "The Concert of Europe". Whatever else it was, this was not a legal institution.

After the end of the 1914/1918 war it was generally recognized that modern warfare had become so horrible that some organised mechanism was required to prevent it. The League of Nations Covenant was the response to this recognition. But it was never effective. The United States and the Soviet Union never joined, and, when it became an inconvenience, Germany pulled out. Apart from the "sanctions" which soon proved ineffective against Italy and Japan, there were no effective "teeth". The whole system disappeared with the outbreak of the Second World War. In 1945, in obedience to the same perception of the need, a more serious attempt at an international order was made by the adoption of the United Nations Charter. This bore, and bears, a greater resemblance to a legally enforceable world order, though it has not prevented numerous military conflicts and confrontations occurring all over the world. Nevertheless, it is at least a beginning. In the first place, it claims to be enforceable against non members. Moreover, subjected always to the "veto", designed by the great powers to preserve their own sovereignty, the Charter possesses a military chapter for imposing military sanctions in the event of serious breach. In the Security Council, but subject always to the "veto", the United Nations Organisation possesses some approach to an executive. It has a permanent seat, a Secretariat, and an "Assembly" though without coercive powers. The old Hague Court has been incorporated as one of the permanent institutions and is the nearest approach so far seen to the creation of an international Court of Justice. But the provisions of the U.N. Charter would not have gone far enough to satisfy my father that anything approaching the minimum requirements of a genuine system of law had been created. Nevertheless, in the fifty years of its existence UNO continues to be relied on by civilised states as the best they can do to achieve some sort of World Order based on the rule of law. It failed to prevent the Cold War prior to the collapse of communism. It has still to face the challenges due to the fragmentation caused by that collapse. Both in the Falklands and the Gulf (neither, arguably, "wars" in the strict sense) it proved its usefulness in cases of clear violations of the Charter. There remain more gaps than one before my father's requirements can be met.

Clearly, one of the most important problems to be faced is the need to control the misuse by sovereign governments of their effective power of repressing or abusing minority groups and cultures within their borders. As I write, the difficulties and failures, whether of UNO or other institutions, to deal with this threat to the rule of law can be illustrated by occurrences in places as different as South Africa, Angola, Korea, Israel, Iraq, and, of course, the Balkans. At the other end of the scale of lawlessness is our failure to combat terrorism as illustrated by the IRA, Lockerbie, or in the Middle East. The need for an acceptable standard of behaviour has clearly not yet been satisfied.

On the credit side, it would be unfair not to mention the growth in Europe and the West, and, in some areas, elsewhere of subordinate groupings such as NATO, EFTA, and the European Community. I do not believe that it is possible to predict what lies ahead. But I believe that the prospects of a new world order are much brighter than they were at the time of the Cuban crisis, and far better than they were in 1945. But the point I wish to make is than any progress and achievement in this field lies in the recognition and enforcement of conduct containing moral value judgments as a means of creating and enforcing an international equivalent of the King's Peace and the institutions necessary to maintain it.

XI The bottom of the Scale. Evil

So far, I have been examining the nature of value judgments from, as it were, the top end of the scale. All value judgments are judgments of quality, good and bad, and, in the relevant sense, quality is always a question of degree. As I said earlier, it is convenient to label the top of the scale 'good' and the bottom of the scale 'bad' or 'evil'. Thus my grandfather's unfinished last letter spoke of 'virtue' and 'vice', 'truth' and 'falsehood', 'kindness' and 'brutality', and we have seen that the aesthetic judgments seem clearly to partake of the same characteristic.

Thus it is convenient to speak of 'beautiful' and 'ugly', 'melodious' and 'cacophonous' with the same sense of working along a two dimensional scale.

But here we come across a curious paradox. When we talk about the 'problem of evil', we are normally really asking ourselves about a problem of metaphysics. We are really asking: 'how can evil coexist in a world created by an all loving, all powerful, and perfectly good God?' But when we talk about the bottom of the scale in connexion with the value judgments, this paradox disappears, and another takes its place. The logical positivists have no difficulty about the first paradox. They have abolished metaphysics as non-sense. Good and Evil are senseless expressions except in so far as they reflect the approval or disapproval of the speaker, and God Himself is a pure hypothesis of which they do not admit the necessity. But the primary thesis which I am seeking to support is that much of the troubles of the present world which occasion in me that feeling of depression with which I began stems from a rejection of the conviction that these value judgments have a real meaning and an objective validity. But when we seek to examine our two dimensional chart, however, the bottom end has a curiously elusive characteristic. Although it may be difficult, even perhaps impossible, to give a precise definition of the words, I believe I know what I mean when I say 'kind', 'true', 'beautiful', 'melodious', and so on. But, as often as not, the bottom of the scale seems to disappear into mist and fog. At the top end of the scale the point of perfection is like the target on a rifle range. There is only one bull's eye, and those qualities or actions which come closest to it score a 'bull', an 'inner', an 'outer' or a 'magpie' in proportion as they come near to hitting the centre of the bull's eye. But, in contrast, there are a million ways of missing the target. There is something entirely negative about a miss. In other words 'good' and 'bad' are not entirely comparable to 'cold' and 'hot'. There is something curiously negative about 'bad'. The same paradox occurs in the Greek language in the word for 'sin' (hamartia) It simply means 'missing the mark'. It has the same characteristic of negation. This is not always the case. It is easy to say of a man that he is 'callous' or 'brutal'. We can also say of a man's face that it is 'ugly', or to use of a human artefact like a picture or a building that it is an 'eyesore', or even a 'carbuncle'. The same curiously negative aspect of evil was observed by some of the medieval theologians who asserted: 'malum est privatio boni' (evil is the absence of good). Is it then the case that our analogy of a sort of two dimensional temperature chart of values needs some revision? In relation to the value judgments, ought we to revise our vocabulary so as, in effect, to retain the conception of 'good', 'true', 'beautiful', 'virtuous', and treat the opposite as something negative, even as non existent? Having lived through the blitz in <u>London</u> and viewed from afar the demonic horror of Hitler's genocide or Stalin's 'evil empire', I find it difficult to go all the way with this. When you come to evaluate acts, judgments, or people with the power of choice, it does not seem to me possible to banish evil simply to the negative idea of something which means no more than the absence of what is positively good. There seems, ineluctably, something which exists and is positively bad. In viewing an occurrence in nature, say a threatening sunset, I may find difficulty in using the word 'ugly'. But I find no difficulty in describing a picture as 'ugly' or a poem as 'obscene'. There is a curious metaphysical point which seems to me to emerge from this line of discussion. In discussing the so-called 'problem of evil' we discerned that this is ordinarily an attempt to answer the question how the existence of evil can be compatible with a good and omnipotent God. I have not myself found it impossible to answer this difficulty, since it does not seem to me inconsistent with the existence of a good and all powerful Deity to suppose that such a Being chose to create a physical world governed by cause and effect and good in itself but containing creatures possessed of free will and thus endowed with the power of choice between good and evil in whatever sense we understand the term. The real questions to which the present enquiry gives rise are, first; whether the existence of the good, the beautiful and the other positive values can be defended without postulating at the same time the existence of a Creator with precisely these characteristics. It is perhaps no coincidence that what led C S Lewis to pass from agnosticism to Theism was precisely his discovery and acceptance of the existence of what he called the Tao. It remains something of an enigma whether the existence of the opposite can be accepted without asserting the purely negative nature of what lies at the bottom end of the scale, or whether the essentially, or at least apparently, demonic characters at present visible in the world of sentient beings does not postulate the existence of some opposite force or personality, like the traditional Satan, to whom Milton attributed the resolution: 'Evil be thou my good'. The problem of evil may be insoluble in a world in which we may see only through a glass darkly. The logical positivist is, of course, not faced with this problem. But, as we have seen, in its dogmatic form, logical positivism is self contradictory.

XII Responsibility.

No-one would attach moral judgments to the motions of a billiard ball or of the electrons surrounding the nucleus of the atom. By contrast, beauty and, less convincingly, ugliness can at times be predicated legitimately of natural objects or phenomena. Greek philosophers even ventured to claim that there was some peculiar virtue in the shape of a sphere which entitled them to draw wholly unjustified conclusions about some natural objects, including the earth itself. But, in addition to the qualitative characteristics to be attributed to them, moral judgments and agents seem to imply a degree of free choice on the part of a conscious agent between alternative courses of action. This is even so when, by analogy, we attempt, by the use of the proverbial sticks and carrots, to train animals not ordinarily regarded as possessing free will in the human sense to do our bidding. To anyone who has ever owned a dog the analogy to human conduct must seem obvious. We would certainly testify to the reality of the apparent reality of their feelings of guilt or satisfaction when, in an appropriate tone of voice, we utter the words "Good boy" or "Bad dog".

To have their effect, however, these words have to be uttered by someone in authority. That is, of course, the essence of the matter. The shepherd's dog acknowledges the voice of the shepherd. Even the sheep know the shepherd's voice and acknowledge the manoeuvres of the dog. The analogy with human conduct is clear. With us, to assert the compulsive force of moral judgment is to acknowledge authority, whether of the "conscience" (whatever that may mean/or the Tao, or the custom, or the government or law, or even the Absolute or an inspired writing or some invisible Godhead. This may be easy in practice so long as the precepts can be formulated or a single source of authority identified and, where necessary, consulted. In real life, difficulties arise when there seem to be rival sources of authority, and sometimes these appear to speak with confused voices. Exact definitions are disputed or missing altogether. Requirements constituting valid claims on our respect may often conflict. Nevertheless, a common factor underlying all moral judgments about conduct is a sense of responsibility to something, some people, or some person. When Immanuel Kant had finished writing the "Critique of pure reason" which asserted the impossibility of knowing the reality of "Things in themselves", he set about writing the "Critique of Practical Reason" which asserted the authority of the Categorical Imperative, that is, of morality. This experience led him to postulate the existence of a personal God who had baffled the searchings of the Pure

Reason when it set out to find him. I am not now concerned to explore the Metaphysics or the Theology of the "Categorical Imperative". What I am concerned to establish is that, though it may be relatively easy to confound the dogmatism of the logical positivist in the way I have attempted its refutation, one is thereby compelled to accept as real our sense of responsibility for the nature of our conduct and the consequences of the actions inspired by our choice of behaviour. The direct corollary of this is to admit an obligation to discern and formulate the kind of conduct which the sense of responsibility is likely to prescribe both in general and in particular cases. This is no easy burden to assume. But to do so postulates the existence of some kind of Authority to whom, or to which, we, as agents, are responsible.

XIII Social Responsibity

We have come a considerable way on our journey. Perhaps the most difficult part was to try to establish that what is really wrong with society in this country, and perhaps elsewhere, is that we have lost our sense of values and the judgments and standards which embody and apply them. As we proceeded on our way, we found that this loss of faith has been associated with what, in intellectual circles is known as logical positivism, and that this doctrine is without foundation and contrary to truth.

Value judgments are not mere noises signifying nothing more than approval or its opposite. They are part of our innate compulsion to rationalise our seemingly not self-explanatory environment. Though not the same as our provisional scientific hypotheses, to which the verification principle applies, they are, in their nature, at least as essentially rational.

The point at which we have arrived is to suggest that a common factor which unites all value judgments in the ethical field is a sense of responsibility to something external to ourselves. We may call this entity the categorical imperative, the Absolute, or, perhaps more simply, God. The purpose of this chapter is to add a new dimension, which I will call a sense of social responsibility.

No doubt it is convenient and in many ways necessary to treat men and women as individuals, islands unto themselves. But, as Aristotle long ago pointed out, man is a gregarious creature, living not only in individual relationships but in subordinate groups, and, above all, in organised societies.

Men and women exist and work in couples, in families, in villages and towns, in factories and workshops and in countless other ways. In actual practice the individual conscience must not only accommodate its behaviour to authority, to law and other individuals, but also to collective groups of all kinds, some natural, like the family, some political, like the state, some voluntary like the Scout movement or the football club. Most important of all men and women are required to develop a sense of corporate duty as members of organised groups both as between these groups and between groups towards individuals outside them. If we read the New Testament attentively, we cannot but be struck by the relatively undeveloped sense of this collective responsibility even at the comparatively late date of the life of the Founder of Christianity. Long before their encounter in the after life, between Dives and Lazarus there was a great gulf fixed. Dives lived in comparative comfort in his dining room. Lazarus picked up scraps under the table among the animals who licked his sores. The young man who departed in discomfiture after being told to go and sell all that he had and give to the poor was in effect being commanded to undertake much of the work which nowadays would be performed by the local authority or the Department of Social Security. Even the Old Testament prophets who, for some purposes, had a very highly developed sense of social responsibility, were mainly concerned with justice between individuals, social and sexual mores, and collective religious observances. It would certainly not be fair to describe primitive or ancient societies as totally unconcerned with the welfare of their members or mutual aid of one sort and another. But, at least in England, it is not unrealistic to date our secular concern for welfare in the modern sense from the dissolution of the monasteries. Examples might be found in the educational foundations under Edward VI and the poor law enacted under Elizabeth I. Apart from privately organised charities, nursing, pensions, and health care on a social scale had to wait for Florence Nightingale and the Liberal Governments of the early twentieth Century. Universal education, again originally the concern of the Churches, was a little earlier in coming, primary universal education dating from the early 1870's and secondary and tertiary education following later at considerable intervals from one another. Anything like welfare provision on the modern scale developed more slowly still. In its present form, it dates from the publication of the Beveridge Report late in 1942, and the legislation of the post war Labour Government, and the debate, both about organisation, means, and ends is by no means over yet. What began as an appeal to the conscience of the individual and the religiously observant when the rich man was bidden to climb through the needle's eye, has ended as a social obligation compulsorily exacted through the rates and taxes by the machinery of the Welfare State.

The weakness of the Welfare State is that it is difficult to discern any coherent philosophy behind it. What is comprehended within the expression "Welfare"? However defined, does Welfare mean a maximum, a minimum, or an average degree of provision in the services provided? Is the provision to be universal or is the assumption that those who are able conveniently to opt out by providing for themselves and their families will, in general, prefer to do so? Is the provision of services to the recipient to be means tested or is it to be automatic? Is the provision to be a sort of negative income tax in favour of the needy? Amongst those who are not so needy are graduated tax concessions envisaged to allow for different sizes of family or marital status?" It needs to be recalled that now, in an age when religious values seem more and more to be in decline, how much of the pioneering work in the field has been due to the influence of Christianity or other religious organisations. The Roman secular state did not quite wash its hands of poorer groups. Small peasant holdings and settlements for retired veterans were encouraged from quite early days. But welfare in the modern sense was largely left to private activities, and though, for more than three centuries, its whole organisation was treated as an illegal conspiracy, the Christian Church was among the pioneers of welfarism. I have already spoken of the medieval monasteries. But, in his book on Late Antiquity, Peter Brown records that, as early as 250 A.D. the urban

Christians of the City of Rome were supporting more than fifteen hundred poor and widows, and were providing ransom for hundreds of Christian captives in Africa and Cappadocia.

When Florence Nightingale started her work in the Crimea it was to nursing orders in Roman Catholic and Protestant Churches that she looked for expertise and skill in what was then virtually an unknown science. The same can be said of a great number of the pioneers in educational and vocational training, and much other social legislation. Noone would seek to minimise the spread, during the nineteenth century in these fields, of people like the Webbs, but the original inspiration came as often as not from men and women like the seventh Earl of Shaftesbury, my own grandfather, Quintin Hogg or his friend and contemporary, Dr. Barnardo. One cannot justly underestimate the direct importance among these of the conception of responsibility, the categorical imperative of charity, which inspired, though not exclusively committed Christians, in creating what is now an almost universal sense of social conscience in a desire to assist what Queen Elizabeth I's legislation are designated as the old, the impotent, (that is the disabled or sick) and the poor and to promote the education of the young. It may be questioned whether, in the absence of religion and religious motives, any of this would have come about.

XIV Where do we go from here?

Does the argument stop here? I began, it will be remembered, in a mood approaching despondency, brought about by the state of the world and the seeming collapse of standards of morality in the United Kingdom. I thought I knew the cause and wished to suggest a remedy. The cause was a lack of belief in the standards of right and wrong, good and bad. I found my enemy in nihilism, the belief that the world in which we live was void of moral values, which means that, despite the achievements of experimental science, and the 'analytic' reasoning of mathematicians, it is basically a tale told by an idiot full of sound and fury and signifying nothing. There are nihilists at both ends of the intellectual scale. It is possible to be a nihilist de facto, and many people are so, not because they are convinced that there is no meaning in life or value in morality to be found, but because they have never given the matter serious consideration at all. At the top end of the scale were the logical positivists. They have reflected on the matter deeply and intelligently. I made these my first target. To them, nihilism is a creed, and, because they believe it to be true, regard its propagation a suitable matter on which to proselytise. I do not believe that they are likely to make many converts because most of us are conscious that making some value judgments all the time is the very stuff of their experience. But the existence at the very top of the intellectual ladder of such an explicit belief is of significance, both because it is very much a sign of the times, and precisely because that belief is an accurate description of the actual code of behaviour by which an increasing number of people live when they are faced with difficult moral decisions. The logical positivist is both intelligent and intellectually honest. I made him my first target because I respect him and wish him to understand why I regard his credo as self contradictory as well as morally destructive. If you believe that judgments about right and wrong are purely subjective noises of approval or disapproval and quite literally non-sense, there can be no basis for moral judgments or decisions at all. There are, of course, those others who, without making any attempt at conscious reflexion on the matter, simply follow the inclinations of the moment without further thought, except, perhaps, a subconscious tendency to be influenced by the conscious incredulity of others. I have attempted to proselytise as little as possible if by proselytisation is meant a conscious effort to propagate my own beliefs about morality or religion. But I have attempted to persuade those who are anxious to give the matter attention that there is nothing vacuous or foolish in saying that the song of a nightingale is beautiful, or that it is better to be kind than cruel, honest than fraudulent, or that it is better to be loyal to friends than to betray them and generally responsible and considerate to others in the field of personal conduct. In that sense only I plead guilty to proselytisation. But I have tried to give reasons for saying that, in holding these beliefs I am using the gift of natural logic with which every normal human being is to some extent endowed and am not simply depending on some supernatural revelation from on high.

But where do we go from here? It is possible, of course, that, in the eyes of the logical positivist, I have only convicted myself of talking nonsense. To those who maintain this I would simply reply that, so far as I know, I have not contradicted myself, as I have tried to show that they have done at the outset of their argument. I would now wish to add that what I have done presents me with not so much a difficulty as a new point of departure. It may be true, I think it is, that there is no way of defining the difference between virtue and vice in terms of something other than themselves or one another; I believe it is also true that, important as general rules and precepts are as a guide to living, the kind of handrail one finds in the Alps to safeguard the walker on a difficult or precipitous path it is never possible to define virtue or vice in terms of precepts or prohibitions to which no possible casuistical exceptions can be found. I have tried to illustrate this by reference to what, perhaps, is the most positive and absolute prohibition of all, that is: "Thou shalt not kill". On examination this turns out to be a lamp to guide our path, and not a lamp post to support our instability. We have to face the questions, old and new, to which the prohibitions and injunctions of conscience and authority give rise, and we may note that new questions are constantly arising. The same may easily be shown to be true of any other rule of conduct which we may seek to adopt for ourselves or which others, wiser than we, have made for us in the past, and to which no lawyer, politician, moral philosopher or private individual can afford to be indifferent. But surely all these difficulties disappear the moment we realise that we are on a pilgrimage and have not arrive, as at first we supposed, at any kind of terminus. For me, at least, a second point is that what we are seeking to follow is not letter but spirit, and that we have found ourselves on an unending journey, guided by lights, warnings and insights as we travel along the road but never by external rules which admit of no exception. Once we have grasped this point it is surely no surprise to learn, and not merely negatively, that the prohibition: "Thou shalt not kill" is not only subject to casuistical exceptions, but, more positively, that the man who permits himself to hate his neighbour without a cause puts himself voluntarily in the same boat as those who literally transgress the prohibition. In the same way, the prohibition against adultery becomes not less, but actually, more binding once it is seen that the sexual instinct is one which in all cases must be monitored responsibly.

But this is not all. There remains the quest for truth, and that is unending. The Universe as we experience it is not self explanatory. The precept to which we have returned: "Thou shalt love thy neighbour as thyself" sets one on an unending pilgrimage of self examination. But even that is not the first, nor the great, commandment. We have still to explore the first, knowing even after pursuing this quest alone we shall not be able to acknowledge an ultimate reality. In this life of pilgrimage we cannot hope to attain it. But we can come for ever closer, in the constantly refined, but always provisional, hypotheses we have to make, whether in our understanding of the physical world, our appreciation of beauty, or in the constant reciprocities and responsibilities of human intercourse. To say that we shall never, within the confines of this life achieve finality is neither to surrender to agnosticism, nor to worship doubt. It is simply to express the result of conviction, trust, and, yes, actual experience as well. For ever, truth is better than falsehood, kindness than brutality, virtue than vice, beauty than ugliness. But what exactly is truth, what falsehood, what exactly in a given context is true kindness, what virtue and what vice are questions to which our hypotheses are never more than provisional, and always subject to revision as we plod our way through the wilderness of experience. Curiously enough, it is at this final point, but with the opposite emphasis, that we approach not all that far from the dogma of the German logical positivist. There comes a point at which we are compelled to say that, as we approach the throne of the ineffable, words fail us. At that stage we are compelled to say with Wittgenstein: "That of which we cannot speak intelligibly is something about which one is bound to keep silence." But it is the silence of worship, not of ignorance.

The End.